Look what I can do

Chris Wildman and Fatima Dike

Illustrated by Marjorie van Heerden

CAMBRIDGE
UNIVERSITY PRESS

Ants in my Pants

I've got ants in my pants!

There's a mouse in my bed!

There's a bat in my hat!

There's a lion in my lap!

Everything's strange,
everything's wrong,
everything's crazy in this funny song!

There's a rhino on my lino.

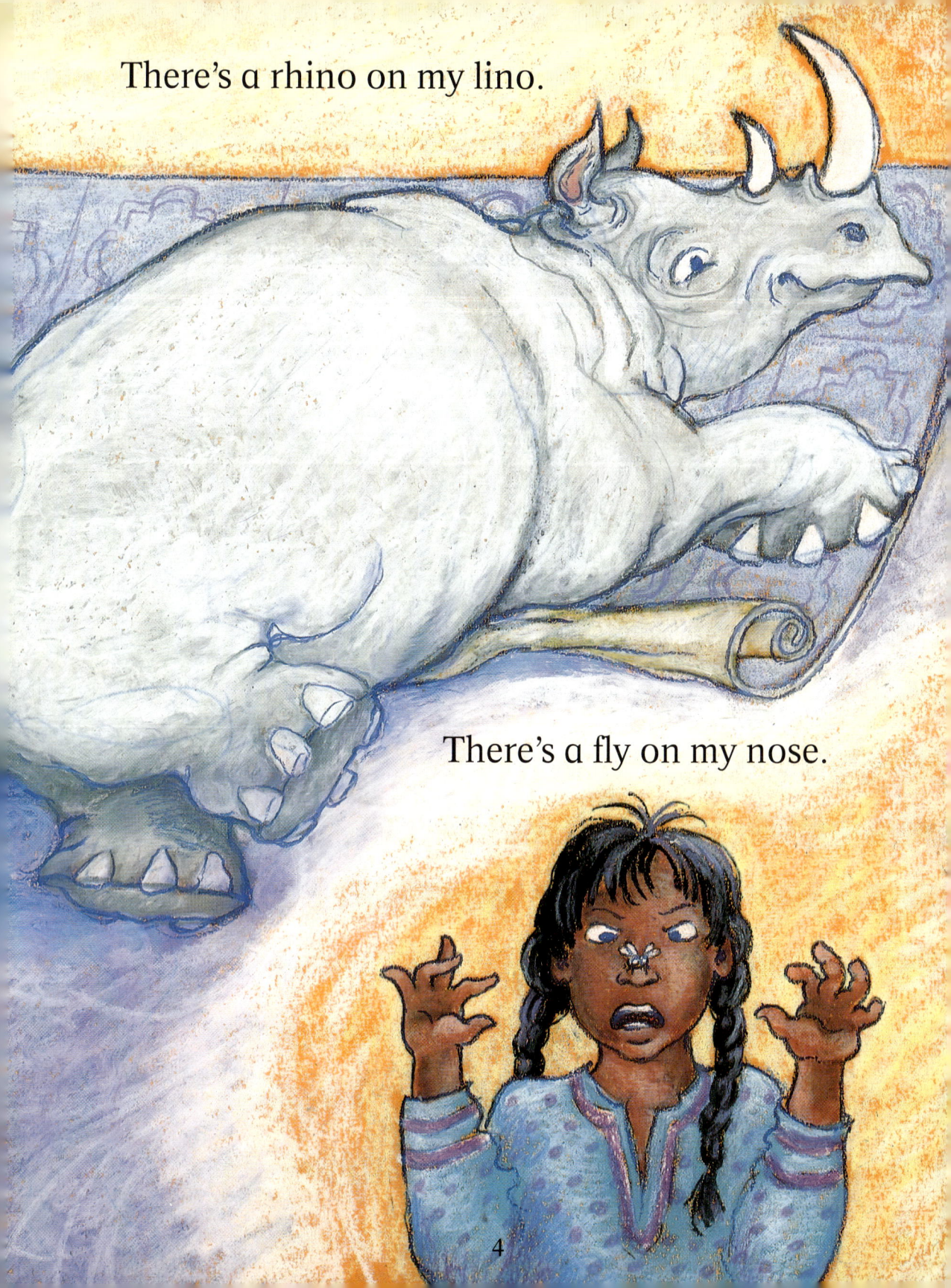

There's a fly on my nose.

There's a parrot on my carrot.

There's a toad on my toes.

Everything's strange,
everything's wrong,
everything's crazy in this funny song!

There's a bear on my chair.

There's a sheep on my shelf.

Now over to you . . .
make the next verse yourself!

Look what I can do

Look what I can do,
I can tie my shoe.
Look what I can do,
you can do it too!

Look how snakes can slide,
on your tummy, on your side.
Look what snakes can do,
you can do it too!

Look how elephants go,
very heavy, very slow.
Look what elephants do,
you can do it too!

Look how monkeys jump,
and land with a bump.
Look what monkeys do,
you can do it too!

Look what I can do,
you can do it too!

Look what I can do,
you can do it too!

Try and catch a Tadpole

Try and catch a tadpole,
swimming in the pond.

Hand full of water,
tadpole gone!

Try and catch a butterfly,
hand be my net.

Hand full of pollen,
is all I get!

Try and catch a cricket,
jumping my way.

Hand full of prickles,
cricket gone away!

Try and catch a frog,
leaping all about.

Almost . . . almost . . . GOT HIM!
Oops! Frog's jumped out!